ICE BREAKERS

60
FUN ACTIVITIES
THAT WILL BUILD A BETTER CHOIR!

By Valerie Lippoldt Mack

To my best friend, Tom,
for being the most patient husband ever.
To my children, Stevie and Zane,
for making every day a new adventure.
To my Butler Headliners, family, and friends,
for blessing me with silver boxes.

Shawnee Press

EXCLUSIVELY DISTRIBUTED BY

HAL•LEONARD®
CORPORATION

7777 W. BLUEMOUND RD. P.O. BOX 13819 MILWAUKEE, WI 53213

Visit Shawnee Press Online at www.shawneepress.com

table of contents

*To indicate that this book is intended for people of both sexes, the
publisher alternates between masculine and feminine pronouns throughout the book.*

ICEBREAKERS

foreword

My parents are music educators and took me to many workshops where I was fortunate to observe master teachers who were extraordinary musicians and educators. At the time, I did not understand or appreciate their life lessons, but now I realize that part of their success was due to their investment and interest in every student.

For many years, I have attempted to create the "perfect" classroom, rehearsal, staff meeting, church choir rehearsal, and even the "perfect" home. It is important to me as a teacher for my students to develop into cohesive groups of people who support and trust each other. By creating and fostering a cooperative experience in and out of the classroom, everyone involved wins. As a director, you must know every student by name and share some sort of common denominator with him or her. How can you understand your students if you do not really know them?

Icebreakers: 60 Fun Activities to Build a Better Choir is a compilation of my favorite activities and games that I have used through out my years of teaching. These exercises are a great way to "break the ice" and allow your students to engage at varying levels of risk to build trust within the ensemble. These simple icebreakers will teach life lessons of respect, tolerance, and patience and your choir will sing differently and develop new connections after playing them. These activities and motivational games are all "kid-tested" in my classroom. Not all students will be ready for certain activities, so I encourage you to allow a voluntary system of participation. Modify any of these activities to fit your situation or classroom.

In a recent rehearsal, the choir was unfocused and the momentum of the rehearsal was moving backwards. Stopping the rehearsal, I asked if anyone had a "High Point Share." Our concert was just days away and the choir members were surprised at the change of direction. One by one, choir members shared positive events that had happened to them during the week. When the choir sang again, the music came alive! We left feeling great about the music and each other because of a 5-minute icebreaker in the middle of a not-so-hot rehearsal.

My profound and humble thanks go out to each of the numerous educators, friends, and family members who have inspired me. May you be blessed for willingly and unselfishly sharing your gifts!

The activities in this book are just the tip of the iceberg when it comes to icebreakers. Be passionate about all you do in and out of your choir and classroom. And always remember…"Ya gotta have heart and music!"

Enjoy…
Valerie Lippoldt Mack

ICEBREAKERS

sing it out

Icebreakers – Just for Fun

PURPOSE:

Sing It Out is a fast and fun icebreaker for students to make new friends. Although some kids may not share information with an entire musical ensemble, they may be comfortable sharing personal facts with just one other person.

REQUIREMENTS:

Slips of paper

PREPARATION:

Predetermine a list of popular song titles. Print or type two copies of each title on the slips of paper, so each person will have a match for his song. (40 students = 20 song titles)

DIRECTIONS:

1. As you hand out the slips of paper, ask the students privately to study the title.
2. Explain that the goal is for the students to find a partner who has the matching song title listed on their slip of paper. Encourage them to move through the room singing the first line of the song loudly. The first couple seated is the winner of this icebreaker.
3. Start the game by saying, "Ready, set, and sing!" Allow sufficient time for the students to move through the room several times searching for their partners.
4. Inform them that once a match is made, the partners sit, introduce themselves, and learn one personal fact about their partner that no one in the group knows.
5. After everyone finds their partners, allow each couple to stand and introduce one another to the rest of the group.

VARIATIONS:

- Instead of partners, try forming larger groups by using fewer song titles. Instead of two people matched up with one song, consider dividing a 100 voice choir with ten songs that will split the choir into equal groups of 10.
- A useful and educational variation is to use a piece of music that your ensemble is rehearsing. Experiment by dividing the song into a verse or a four-bar phrase. The students will sing or play their assigned measures in effort of finding others singing the same phrase.

ICE TIPS:

- Select titles from nursery rhymes, holiday songs, patriotic selections, disco favorites, folk songs, radio top 40, or selections that you are currently studying.
- This icebreaker can be a lesson on understanding and appreciating diversity. Students may discover one person's favorite music is another person's least favorite music. Discuss how boring our world would be if we could only listen to or perform one style of music.
- This fun icebreaker teaches singers to project and enjoy making music. What's more, everyone in the school will literally hear how fun it is to be a member of your music ensemble!

ICEBREAKERS

PURPOSE:
It Takes Two gives the class an opportunity to spend time with others they do not know well. The instructor can assist in matching partners and creating communication between choir members.

REQUIREMENTS:
One sticky note for each member of the class

PREPARATION:
Write the names of famous "pairs" on sticky notes. Some examples of famous twosomes are Laurel and Hardy, Abbott and Costello, Romeo and Juliet, Martin and Lewis, Ben and Jerry, Laverne and Shirley, Sonny and Cher, or Thelma and Louise.

DIRECTIONS:
1. Place sticky notes on each student's back with instructions not to look at the note.
2. Instruct the participants to find the partner of their famous pair. They can accomplish this by asking other classmates questions about the name on their backs. Classmates can respond using only "yes" or "no" answers.
3. Once finding the other half of their pair, the students sit, introduce themselves, and discuss their matching pair.
4. If there are an odd number of students, the accompanist should participate.

VARIATIONS:
- **Non-Verbal It Takes Two** Play this icebreaker only using non-verbal communication; i.e. hand gestures and facial expressions.
- Try inanimate pairs such as salt and pepper, peanut butter and jelly, sun and moon, macaroni and cheese, shoes and socks, or ketchup and mustard.
- Allow the students to brainstorm a list of pairs to use for future classes.

ICE TIP:
Use this opportunity to turn the icebreaker into a historical lesson of pairs (Mozart and Salieri, Tchaikovsky and *The Nutcracker Suite*, Lewis and Clark, or Fred and Ginger).

beach ball blast-off

Icebreakers – Just for Fun

PURPOSE:
The goal of the *Beach Ball Blast-Off* is to keep the ball in the air as long as possible without allowing it to touch the floor. This is a fun and lively activity that encourages goal setting, teamwork, hand-eye coordination, and listening skills.

REQUIREMENTS:
Beach balls or balloons

PREPARATION:
None

DIRECTIONS:
1. Divide the class into groups of three to eight members.
2. Toss a beach ball or balloon out into the group and instruct them to keep it in the air. The students can only use their hands to hit the ball or balloon. If the same person hits the ball two times in a row or the ball touches the floor, the score drops to zero.
3. Ask the students to count aloud to score how many times the group can hit it before it touches the floor.
4. Aim for highest points to see which team can reach its goal.

VARIATIONS:
- For an unpredictable game, add water to the inside of the beach ball.
- For a more stimulating challenge, throw out multiple beach balls at any one time.
- Limit the group to hitting the ball with only the body part called out (knees, elbows, heads, feet, etc.).
- **Ice-Ball** Create a variation by using 100 Headliner Questions to cover the beach balls with the questions (found on pages 51-52). Although this takes some prep time, keep in mind that by using permanent ink, the Ice-Ball will last for many years. As the student catches the ball, he must introduce himself and answer the question that is touching his left thumb. The game continues as the Ice-Ball is tossed to another student

ICE TIP:
Beach Ball Blast-Off has the potential to become a competitive contact activity.

shoe shopping

PURPOSE:
Shoe Shopping is a fun way for students to follow directions and try something new, while learning a fun fact about each person. "...On with the shoe!"

REQUIREMENTS:
Shoes the students are wearing

PREPARATION:
None

DIRECTIONS:
1. Ask students to take off their right shoe and place them in a pile.
2. Have students sit in a large circle.
3. When you say "Shoe Shop," all students stand and grab someone else's shoe.
4. Inform the students to return to their place in the circle, sit, and try the shoe on. If their selected shoe is too small, they can put it on their right hand.
5. Share that the goal is for the student to stand in front of the person who is wearing the matching shoe and form a circle. Once a match is made, the students should make introductions and discuss their favorite footwear; e.g. tennis shoes, flip-flops, designer brands, football cleats, bowling shoes, or no shoes at all.

VARIATIONS:
- If it is a cold winter day, substitute mittens or stocking caps.
- Designate a hat day and use baseball caps, winter hats, cowboy hats, etc. Instead of matching shoes, the student finds the person belonging to the hat and forms a circle.

ICE TIPS:
- Try to do this activity on a day when students will not be wearing matching shoes.
- This activity is more energizing than real shoe shopping and it only takes minutes instead of hours!

I C E B R E A K E R S

human words

Icebreakers – Just for Fun

PURPOSE:
The *Human Words* exercise requires participants to move quickly while listening to the instructor.

REQUIREMENTS:
Stopwatch

PREPARATION:
Prepare a list of words.

DIRECTIONS:
1. The instructor gives each group a word.
2. Instruct the students that the entire group must spell the given words with their bodies by lying on the floor. Score points according to speed. If space is available, the groups can go at the same time. If space is limited, time each group with the stopwatch to determine who has the fastest time.

VARIATIONS:
- Instead of providing a single word, the instructor furnishes a small sentence for the assignment. The group must figure out who is taking each part of the word, as well as spelling the word correctly.
- **Human Riddle** The instructor asks the class a riddle. Each group must first solve the riddle and then spell out the answer with their bodies.
- **Standing Human Words** The icebreaker is played the same with the exception of standing up to create the words.

ICE TIP:
This icebreaker game could serve as a cross curricular activity with another department.

ICEBREAKERS

fortune cookies "...on stage"

PURPOSE:
This fun and delicious icebreaker encourages positive visualization.

REQUIREMENTS:
One fortune cookie with a fortune inside for each participant

PREPARATION:
Create fortune cookies with personal messages that directly relate to your school, your music program, and your students. If you have an ambitious parent committee, ask volunteers to make the cookies and stuff them with the fortunes.

DIRECTIONS:
1. Ask the students to sit in a circle.
2. Hand each student a fortune cookie.
3. Direct the students to break open their fortune cookies to find a message.
4. Ask the students to go around the circle, reading their fortune and adding the phrase "...on stage!"
5. Create discussion about the most inspiring fortunes and the silliest fortunes. Raise the question of which fortunes did not make sense.

Three fortune examples:
- You will have great success ... on stage!"
- Be sure you do not look backwards ... on stage!"
- Nothing great was ever achieved without a positive attitude and enthusiasm ... on stage!"

VARIATION:
Candy Fortunes Try a variation with Valentine candy hearts. Pre-select the candy messages to prevent an embarrassing situation (avoid "Be mine ... on stage!" fortunes.) Mini-candy bars with statements on the inside of the wrappers also work well. Smaller treats are more cost effective.

ICE TIPS:
- This fun activity is different every time you play the game. Put some thought into composing clever fortunes.
- Elementary students can practice reading skills with this activity.
- Do this icebreaker when the singers are ready for a sugar-boost!

ICEBREAKERS

no smiling please!

Icebreakers – Just for Fun

PURPOSE:
No Smiling, Please! challenges the participants' control of their minds, bodies, and faces.

REQUIREMENTS:
None

PREPARATION:
None

DIRECTIONS:
1. Explain to the class that the sole purpose of this activity is to make the chosen student laugh, smirk, or lose control. The leader may use voice fluctuations, body language, or facial expressions to affect the targeted student.
2. Ask a volunteer to start. That student chooses a classmate, looks her in the eye and says, "Baby, I love you, but I just can't make you smile." If the targeted student reacts in any way (a laugh, a smile, a grimace, etc.), she is eliminated and moves to the front of the room to watch. The volunteer then moves onto another target and repeats the process.
3. If the targeted student is able to refrain from reacting, he or she is declared the winner of that round.

VARIATION:
Group No Smiling, Please Line the students in two rows, asking them to stand back-to-back. Caution the students to remain serious and avoid cracking a smile. On the count of three, the students turn to face their partner. The first student of the pair to smile is eliminated and sits down. The winners of that round find a new partner for the next round of competition. The most "serious" student is the winner.

ICE TIPS:
- Acting skills will play a part in this icebreaker.
- A few focused students will be able to maintain their composure while others will go into hysterics.
- Allow the eliminated students to smile, laugh, and comment from the sidelines.

silent line drills

PURPOSE:
This activity encourages students to feel comfortable with one another and their new environment as they learn personal trivia about their classmates.

REQUIREMENTS:
None

PREPARATION:
None

DIRECTIONS:
1. Explain that group members should silently arrange themselves in the order directed (see sample topics below).
2. When the group has completed the task, they should sit down in their line.
3. Ask the students to go down the line to state their name and announce how they fit in the line based on the directive given. For example, you could ask them to line up according to birth dates. A student born on January 1st stands at the head of the line and a student born on December 31st will be at the tail of the line. The rest of the students silently arrange themselves according to the month and day they were born.

Example topics for Silent Line Drills:
- Shoe size (Smallest to largest; include 1/2 sizes)
- Alphabetical first, middle, or last name (helpful grade book alphabetization)
- Address numbers (smallest to largest numbers)
- Bowling scores (lowest to highest bowling score ever received)
- Secret family recipe (how many ingredients are used)
- Height (shortest to tallest; this is a helpful exercise to determine robe, costume, or uniform assignments)
- Voicing (lowest voice to the highest voice)
- Hair length or hair color (shortest to longest or lightest to darkest)
- Favorite ice cream flavor (alphabetically)

VARIATION:
Use a stopwatch to time the activity. Repeat this icebreaker over a semester, trying to improve the class' time with each recurring game.

ICE TIPS:
- The silent line drills are great exercises in self-control, non-verbal communication skills are improved, and the students work together to achieve the same goal.
- Repeat this icebreaker on a weekly basis with minor modifications for variety.

ICEBREAKERS

musical categories

Icebreakers – Just for Fun

PURPOSE:
Musical Categories is a competitive icebreaker, allowing participants to take risks in a smaller class or group setting while working towards a common goal.

REQUIREMENTS:
Note cards

PREPARATION:
Predetermine a list of up to ten topics (see examples provided below).

DIRECTIONS:
1. Divide the students into teams.
2. Instruct a volunteer from the first team to choose a note card and announce the topic to the entire class.
3. Allow the teams 15 seconds to discuss the topic on the card and collectively decide on a song that mentions the topic. At the end of the allotted time, the first group must sing one line of a song that mentions the topic. For example, a chosen note card says, "Transportation." At the end of 15 seconds, the group members sing, "Row, Row, Row Your Boat." The second group must sing a different song that mentions the same topic. The groups continue to take turns presenting their different songs that have a common topic. If a group is unable to come up with a line from a song, they lose that round and the other teams are awarded a point.
4. Play until you reach a certain score or time runs out.

    Example Topics for *Musical Categories*:
    - Days of the Week
    - Jewelry or "Bling"
    - Names (boys', girls' or nicknames)
    - Cities, states, or countries
    - Colors
    - Food
    - Animals
    - Numbers
    - Directions (up, down, over, around, outside)
    - Holidays

VARIATION:
Invite your principal, accompanist, or booster parents to play the game with your class, bringing in different generations and players' perspectives.

ICE TIPS:
- This icebreaker is a great reminder that music is fun. Participants should not worry about their sound. Give them permission to sing out and enjoy making music with friends!
- Childhood songs, campfire songs, top songs off the radio, and commercial jingles will bring back many memories for the participants.

ICEBREAKERS

melody chaos

PURPOSE:

Students must work closely together to achieve the end goal. The students will gain the realization that everyone plays a role in a successful task.

REQUIREMENTS:

Puzzle pieces for the melody
Stopwatch

PREPARATION:

Compose a short melody and create a puzzle of the melodic phrase (Create as many puzzle pieces as you have participants. If the group is large, divide the participants into teams and have a competition between the groups).

DIRECTIONS:

1. Hand each student a piece of the puzzle.

2. Instruct the students to work together to put the puzzle together.

3. Time the students to see how quickly they can finish the puzzle.

VARIATIONS:

- Instead of a melody, substitute a composer photo, the ensemble's group photo, a comic strip, or a cardboard puzzle.
- **Pumpkin Chaos** A great activity for a fall retreat is to substitute a pumpkin for the melody puzzle. Prior to class, scoop out the inside of the pumpkin and cut the pumpkin shell into several pieces. Instruct students to use toothpicks to piece the pumpkin back together. Create a competition between several groups to see who can successfully put the pieces of the pumpkin back together the quickest. Use newspaper or a tablecloth for your workspace.

ICE TIP:

Lead a discussion that compares the ensemble to a puzzle. Like a puzzle piece, each student is unique and important. When one piece is missing, the puzzle is incomplete. Every person has a specific job and if a role is not covered, the entire program suffers. No job or puzzle piece is too small or insignificant when it comes to achieving the final goal.

take as much as you think you need

Icebreakers – Just for Fun

PURPOSE:
Students will discover personal information about their peers (likes, dislikes, hobbies, etc).

REQUIREMENTS:
A roll of unused toilet paper

PREPARATION:
None

DIRECTIONS:
1. Pass a roll of toilet paper around a circle of students.
2. Tell students, "Take as much as you think you will need, but no more than ten squares."
3. After everyone has torn off their squares, inform the students that the objective of this icebreaker is to share one interesting fact about himself for each square of toilet paper.
4. If the student is unable to think of a fact, take this opportunity to quiz her favorite musical number, hobby, soda, fast food, subject in school, radio station, etc.

VARIATIONS:
- Disperse multiple colored sticky notes. While the students think they will be taking notes, surprise them by asking each student to share personal information associated with each color. This variation gives them the opportunity to teach.
- Give students four or five pieces of colored candy. Each color represents personal information they must share about themselves.

Color Categories and Statements for the Variations:
- Red - Share something with which you are passionate.
- Green - Share an embarrassing moment.
- Yellow - Say something positive about someone in the circle.
- Orange - Share the title of a favorite song.
- All other colors - Eat the candy without sharing any information.

ICE TIP:
Although a silly exercise, the icebreaker encourages discussions about the spirited people and the fun activities in the Fine Arts Department.

I C E B R E A K E R S

jammin' name game

PURPOSE:
This icebreaker allows creativity with simple choreography and the English language while participants learn each other's names while movin' and groovin'.

REQUIREMENTS:
None

PREPARATION:
None

DIRECTIONS:
1. Ask students to stand in a large circle (This activity works best for groups of 10-25 people. If there are more people, break them into smaller circles).
2. Direct the students to think of an adjective that begins with the same letter or sound as their first name. They also need to think of a simple action or choreography that relates to the adjective they chose. For example, "Grinning Greg" (pointing to his dimples), "Zany Zane" (wildly waving her hands in the air), or "Vivacious Valerie" (energetically wiggling spirit fingers). The adjectives must be positive; do not allow descriptions like "Stupid Steve" or "Dumb David."
3. Start the game by introducing yourself with your adjective and choreography. Move the game to the person to your right.
4. The second person in line repeats the first person's adjective, name, and demonstrates the choreography associated with it and then follow with his own adjective, name, and choreography. The third person in line repeats the information from the previous two and then adds her own adjective, name, and action.
5. Continue going around the circle until everyone has had a turn. Everyone in the circle should be able to repeat each person's name, adjective, and matching action.

VARIATION:
Students perform the action and classmates have to guess the adjective that matches their movement. Make this task easier by stating that the adjectives must start with the same letter as the first name.

ICE TIPS:
- This is one of the fastest ways to learn all of the students' names. It really works! You will see innovative and fun choreography as students introduce themselves.
- Choir members will enjoy the rehearsals more and feel a part of the ensemble when they are addressed by their first names (instead of, "Hey, you!" across the classroom).
- The participants need to be creative and willing to meet new people.

paper sky transporters

Communication Builders – Getting to Know You

PURPOSE:
This icebreaker challenges the group to communicate verbally and to improve listening skills.

REQUIREMENTS:
Blank pieces of paper (One 8 1/2" x 11" piece for every two people in the group)

PREPARATION:
None

DIRECTIONS:
1. Ask class members to stand back-to-back with a partner.
2. The pair should designate who is the describer and who is the listener.
3. Give the listener an 8 1/2" x 11" piece of paper with instructions that he will be folding an inanimate object.
4. Secretly instruct the describer to explain clearly how to make a paper airplane. (It is important the listener does not know the end result should be a paper airplane.)
5. When the partners are finished, ask the pair to face each other. While some of the listeners may have understood the directions and folded an airplane, it will be humorous to see what other designs were produced.
6. After the reactionary chuckles from the students, lead a discussion about describing and listening.

VARIATION:
Continue the challenge by holding a paper airplane contest to see if any of the airplanes can fly (aim for a trashcan).

ICE TIPS:
Discussion questions for this simple and fun airplane exercise:
- Ask the students to discuss if the describing or listening role was easier.
- How important is visualization when working on a project?
- How confident must a describer be when giving directions?
- If one detail is missed, the project may not "fly."
- As musicians, is it hard to create without visualizing the final product?
- How do composers create without visualizing a finished project?

three letters that best describe you

Communication Builders – Getting to Know You

PURPOSE:

This game will stimulate creative thinking and encourage personal interaction.

REQUIREMENTS:

Alphabetical list of topics (see examples below)

PREPARATION:

None

DIRECTIONS:

1. Choose three letters for the day.

2. Decide on a subject that starts with those letters (for example, A-animals, B-books, and C-cartoon characters) See the list below or compose your own alphabetical list and categories.

3. Explain that the students should choose an animal (A), book (B), and cartoon character (C) that best describe them, which they most identify with, and why they made that choice.

4. Require the students to share only positive answers

Category ideas for *Three Letters That Best Describe You:*

A	Animal	N	Newspaper section
B	Book	O	Object from your locker
C	Cartoon	P	Parent
D	Dancer	Q	Quote that describes you
E	Eggs (how cooked?)	R	Radio station
F	Fast food item	S	Singer
G	Gadget	T	Tree
H	Hairstyle	U	Unique fact
I	Instrument	V	Vehicle
J	Jewel	W	Website
K	Keepsake	X	"X-tra" special role model
L	Light (candle, fluorescent, bulb)	Y	Yoga pose (warrior, tree, dead bug)
M	Movie that describes your life	Z	Zodiac sign

VARIATIONS:

- Use this icebreaker as a writing assignment. Ask students to write their answers quickly and turn them in at the beginning of class. You can share results at another time or give the assignment back at the end of the grading period.

- Use this icebreaker as a small group project, asking the students to discuss their answers with one another.

ICE TIP:

Challenge your students to brainstorm as a group to compose a new list of unique and interesting categories.

ICEBREAKERS

tennis ball tango

Communication Builders – Getting to Know You

PURPOSE:

This icebreaker teaches students to pay attention and think on their feet. Class members must stay focused or they may be hit by a tennis ball. The students will definitely know their classmates' names by the end of the game!

REQUIREMENTS:

Tennis balls
Ball of yarn (for variation)

PREPARATION:

None

DIRECTIONS:

1. Instruct the students to stand in a circle.

2. Give one student a tennis ball.

3. Explain the directions. The student says a name of a person who is in the circle and tosses the tennis ball to that student. After the second person catches the ball, she tosses the ball to another student while saying his name. Students should not return the tennis ball back to the person who tossed it to them. The game gets faster and more exciting as up to five tennis balls are added. Start this game slowly and do not add additional tennis balls until the group is successful with a single tennis ball.

VARIATIONS:

- **Spider Web Tango** Using a big ball of yarn, repeat the above instructions. Tell the students to stay connected with the group by holding on to their portion of the yarn.

- **Reverse Spider Web Tango** Add another twist by instructing the members to reverse the pattern of the yarn, complete with names, so the group can untangle themselves. The group will be a part of a messy spider web if the students do not remember the exact order.

ICE TIP:

This icebreaker and its variations challenge hand-eye coordination and definitely keep class members on their toes. In addition, this game will help students learn their classmates' names in a non-threatening and fun manner.

PURPOSE:

Students work in small groups and listen to each other. This is a great way to for students to show what they really know and what is a preconceived idea regarding their music director. After this exercise, students will be better acquainted with their instructor.

REQUIREMENTS:

Quiz (questions should all pertain to the instructor)
Writing utensil

PREPARATION:

- Prepare a quiz about the instructor, choir director, accompanist, etc.
- At the beginning of the week, announce that there will be quiz on the last day of the week. Suggest students pay attention throughout the week so they will ace the quiz. Avoid telling the class that all the questions will be about the teacher.

DIRECTIONS:

1. Divide the students into groups of three to five members.
2. Instruct the groups to answer the quiz questions. A majority of facts about the instructor have not been discussed during class time.
3. At the end of the quiz, read the questions aloud and give the correct answers.
4. Grade each exam to determine how well each group knows the teacher.
5. Ask if any group received a perfect score.

Ideas for Questions: (These are some quiz questions used in my classroom, but tailor the questions around what you want your students to learn about you).

- What is the last book your instructor has read?
- What is your instructor's favorite fast food? Favorite homemade food?
- Who is your instructor's favorite singer? Favorite music group?
- Who is your instructor's least favorite singer? Least favorite group?
- What does your instructor do in her free time?
- What TV programs does your instructor watch?
- What is your instructor's favorite movie or type of movie?
- Who is your instructor's inspiration in life?
- What are three of your instructor's biggest pet peeves?
- List something you could do in class to help your instructor?

VARIATION:

Instead of a group activity, hand out the quiz to each student.

ICE TIP:

It is entertaining to learn what your students think they know about you.

see and say

Communication Builders – Getting to Know You

PURPOSE:

This icebreaker is an excellent observation game and a lesson in picking up details. It takes a few minutes to play but the impact of the lesson will be remembered for a long time.

REQUIREMENTS:

None

PREPARATION:

Determine the actions you will announce.

DIRECTIONS:

1. Explain the directions while the students rise to a standing position.
2. Announce a verbal direction as you perform it (for example, touch your nose). As quickly as possible, students should carry out the directive given by the teacher.
3. Calculate reaction times.
4. On the last statement, perform a different action than the verbal direction given to see who was listening and who was merely mimicking (instead of touching your nose, touch your forehead). The students should not be aware of this trickery.
5. Survey the room to see how many followed the verbal directions and how many followed the non-verbal action.

> **Directives for *See and Say*:** (demonstrate each action as you announce each)
> - Put your hands on your knees.
> - Clap your hands three times.
> - Fold your arms.
> - Stamp your right foot two times.
> - Shrug your shoulders.
> - Bend down to touch your toes.
> - Touch your fingers behind your back.
> - Balance on your left leg.
> - Touch your nose (on the last statement, instead of touching your nose, touch your forehead).

VARIATIONS:

- Use musical examples from your choir repertoire to vary this icebreaker.
- If you are using movement in rehearsals, students need to pay attention to what is said as well as what is demonstrated non-verbally.
- Teach students to remain focused and to avoid the "automatic pilot" stare!

ICE TIP:

Discuss how actions can speak louder than words. How does this statement pertain to your class? How does that statement fit into life situations outside of school? Ask the class members to provide examples of actions speaking louder than words.

ICEBREAKERS

get an autograph

PURPOSE:
Participants learn each other's names in a creative manner.

REQUIREMENTS:
Quiz
Writing Utensils

PREPARATION:
Prepare a quiz for each participant.
(Use the sample quiz below or create an exam with specific interview questions representing the talents and interests of your students).

DIRECTIONS:
1. Pass out the quiz and pencils. Ask students to turn the quiz downward until everyone in the class has received the document.
2. Give the instructions. Each student is on a quest to find a student who fits each description and asks him to autograph that line. The goal is to find a different person for each description. A person cannot give his autograph twice to the same person. The first person to have the entire quiz finished is the winner!

Ideas for *Get an Autograph*:
Find someone who...
_____ is left-handed.
_____ squeezes the toothpaste tube from the middle.
_____ loves algebra.
_____ hates chocolate.
_____ has a collection (include the type of collection).
_____ can speak a foreign language.
_____ can sing all the lyrics to "Copacabana."
_____ has stayed in a hospital within the past year.
_____ sings in a community or church choir.
_____ can milk a cow.
_____ has traveled overseas.
_____ writes poetry.
_____ likes to sew.
_____ has a pet at home (include the pet's name).
_____ has met a famous person (include the person's name).

VARIATION:
Ask the class to brainstorm questions for future *Get An Autograph* games.

ICE TIP:
Finding other people in the class who have a unique quality gives the students a sense of belonging while providing valuable information about students.

15 second musical share

Communication Builders – Getting to Know You

PURPOSE:
This icebreaker challenges the group to communicate thoughts and feelings, as well as improve listening skills. These skills are of utmost importance!

REQUIREMENTS:
None

PREPARATION:
Ask the students to think of "Musical Shares" that could be discussed with little notice.

DIRECTIONS:
1. Explain a "Musical Share" is to introduce one's self and tell the class of a musical passion he has or something musical he has done that no one else in the class can claim to have done.
2. Be prepared to coach and remind the students of successes at past rehearsals, class meetings, performances, travels, and favorite childhood examples.
   Tell the students that if someone has already shared a specific musical experience, the person must think of something else to share.
3. Volunteer to go first and to give an example of a "Musical Share."
4. Continue passing the "Musical Share" around the class until everyone has had a turn.

VARIATIONS:
- Invite students to bring ticket stubs, program books, photos, short videos, scrapbook pages, or sheet music as a visible symbol of their musical share.
- This activity could extend over the course of a week or a semester. If spreading this activity over an entire semester, allow only a few students during each class period to reveal their "Musical Share."

ICE TIPS:
- *Musical Share* is an effective way to get students to open up in front of a group of their peers. Allowing a student to talk about something he is passionate about is less intimidating than having to speak on a subject about which he knows little.
- The next time the student wants to audition for a solo or a speaking part, the risk may not be so difficult. Often times, it is more challenging to speak to a group of peers than it is to make a presentation to a room of strangers.
- It may be surprising to learn what makes a difference and what matters most in a student's life. Sometimes a challenging piece of music on the "most-hated list" turns into the "most-favorite of all time" by the end of the year. Many times, instructors are completely unaware of the change of tide.

name origin

PURPOSE:

This communication builder will immediately involve students in discussion, helping the students get acquainted and learning interesting facts about each other, while shifting the focus from the teacher and the material to the student.

REQUIREMENTS:

None

PREPARATION:

None

DIRECTIONS:

1. Ask volunteers to introduce themselves and to share the origin of their name (allow them to choose between their first, middle, last name, or even nickname).

2. Lead a discussion about personal choices regarding names with the entire class or in smaller sub-groups.
   - What are some names you would choose for yourself instead of your given name?
   - What names would you choose for your own children?
   - What names of famous people in history do you admire?

3. Lead a discussion about the name of the choir or ensemble with the entire class or in smaller sub-groups.
   - What significance is the name of your choir or ensemble?
   - Does the name of the group fit the ensemble?
   - Do the current members uphold the traditions of past groups?
   - Is the group keeping the same standards as former groups?

VARIATION:

Similar to researching a family tree, students could research the school's music history as an extra credit project, creating a musical scrapbook about music ensembles, distinguished alumni, community performers, local garage bands all hailing from the same alma mater. This kind of a presentation would come in handy if your school has a strong alumni association or celebrates reunions.

ICE TIP:

A student can exhibit so much passion and pride when discussing family history and childhood years. There may be a student who does not feel comfortable revealing any personal information and barely contributes in group discussions. This subject matter may generate discussion from some of your more reserved students.

ICEBREAKERS

silent salutations

Communication Builders – Getting to Know You

PURPOSE:
Participanats must learn as much as they can about each student using only non-verbal cues.

REQUIREMENTS:
Chalkboard or dry erase board
Chalk or markers

PREPARATION:
Write three or four questions on the chalkboard or dry erase board that you would like students to learn about one another.

DIRECTIONS:
1. Instruct the students to meet and greet one another without talking.
2. Ask the individuals to circulate through the class and introduce themselves to each person with some sort of physical greeting, e.g. handshake, smile, head nod, high-five, hug, or a wave.

   Possible questions for Silent Salutations:
   - Your name
   - Instrument you play
   - Part you sing in the choir
   - Your favorite musical group
   - Your favorite song from the choir folder
   - What is your next class? What was your last class?

VARIATIONS:
Added Gratitude Ending each rehearsal on a positive note is a great habit to establish for your classroom. One way is for the students silently to thank their folder partner or the person standing next to them with a high-five, a thumbs-up, a peace out, or any type of silent action.

ICE TIPS:
- While students are exchanging information with each other, the instructor can enjoy a few minutes of planning time.
- *Silent Salutations* is a great icebreaker to strengthen students' very important non-verbal communication skills.

ICEBREAKERS

pop quiz

PURPOSE:

Pop Quiz is a "getting-to-know-you" icebreaker that is a physical activity.

REQUIREMENTS:

Balloons
Helium (optional)
Slips of paper

PREPARATION:

Write generic questions on the slips of paper and slide them inside the balloon while inflating.

DIRECTIONS:

1. Give each student a balloon.

2. One at a time, allow the students to pop their balloons to access the slip of paper.

3. Once the balloon pops, the student reads the question on the slip of paper aloud and answers it.

   ### Sample questions for *Pop Quiz*:
   - Favorite exercise
   - What fast food could you not live without
   - A fictional character you would like to meet
   - Favorite breakfast cereal
   - Childhood dream
   - My perfect date
   - My favorite sport and college team
   - Favorite activity on a free weekend

VARIATIONS:

- To add an element of competition, two students can sit on their balloons to see who can pop it first.
- Allow students to work together to pop a balloon between their bodies.
- Limit the ways that students can pop their balloons (sitting on them, squeezing with their hands, etc.)
- If you need to keep the noise level down, write the question on the outside of several balloons with a marker. Throw the balloons in the air and give students ten seconds to grab a balloon. Whoever captures a balloon first answers the question aloud. Continue until everyone has answered the question.

ICE TIP:

This activity is fun and entertaining to observe.

I C E B R E A K E R S

rock, opera, disco

Energizers – Stress Reducers and Let's Get Physical

PURPOSE:
Similar to "Rock, Paper, Scissors," participants can let their hair down, roll up their pants, and have lots of fun in *Rock, Opera, Disco*.

REQUIREMENTS:
Chalkboard or dry erase board
Chalk or dry erase markers

PREPARATION:
Write the scoring matrix on the chalkboard or dry erase board
- Rock wins over Opera
- Opera wins over Disco
- Disco wins over Rock

DIRECTIONS:
1. Instruct the students to stand back-to-back with a partner.
2. Tell them to decide which of the three poses below that they will present.
    Rock Star (Hands lifted above head, fingers in a heavy metal pose)
    Opera Singer (Hands clasped in front of chest in an opera stance)
    Disco (Pose with index finger pointed in the air, i.e. 1970s John Travolta)
3. On the count of three, the students turn to face their partner in their chosen stance (Repeat the exercise if both members of the pair choose the same pose).
4. Refer students to the posted scoring matrix and ask them to determine the winner.
5. Continue the competition as winners compete against other winners until you have one winner in the class.

VARIATION:
Ninjas, Cowboys, and Godzilla This variation is similar to *Rock, Opera, Disco,* except the students add their own vocal inflections associated with a ninja, cowboy, or Godzilla. Determine the scoring matrix before beginning.
    Ninja (Strike a karate pose and screech, "Hi-yah!")
    Cowboy (Grab buckle and imaginary hat and twang, "Yee-haw!")
    Godzilla (Sway arms above head and bellow, "Ahhh!")

ICE TIP:
Tell the class they have your permission to enjoy this icebreaker by acting ridiculous. Encourage them to go with their first inclination and to not think too hard about how they will pose.

laughing game

PURPOSE:

The Laughing Game reduces stress and energizes students on those days when no one, including the instructor, feels like rehearsing.

REQUIREMENTS:

None

PREPARATION:

None

DIRECTIONS:

1. Ask the class to sit in a circle.
2. Explain that the participants pass the word, "Ha!" around the circle in a controlled and calm manner.
3. Start the process by saying the word, "Ha!"
4. Pass it to the next person on your right who echoes "Ha!" and adds his own "Ha!"
5. The next person to his right inserts another "Ha!" resulting in a "Ha, ha, ha!"
6. Continue the icebreaker around the circle with each person adding another "Ha!" while maintaining her composure.
7. End the game when the "Ha, ha, ha's!" have gone completely around the circle.

VARIATIONS:

- Substitute the silly words, "Tee-hee," "Yuk," "Hardy-har," or "Giggle" for "Ha!"
- Assess proper breath technique with your singers by asking them to lie on their backs on the floor while saying their "Ha's" "forcing them to breathe correctly from their diaphragms.
- *Stack It Up Laughing Game* The first person lies on his back on the floor. The second person places his head on the first person's stomach. The third person places his head on the second person's stomach and so on. If a group is larger than 24 individuals, break them into smaller groups.

ICE TIPS:

- *Laughing Game* is a wonderful exercise for students to check their breathing technique.
- It is nearly impossible to stay in a bad mood after this laughing icebreaker!

ICEBREAKERS

bean bag toss

Energizers – Stress Reducers and Let's Get Physical

PURPOSE:

The *Bean Bag Toss* is a great way to check if students are alert and understanding the material that has been covered. Perform this icebreaker with the entire class to make sure that every one comprehends the subject matter.

REQUIREMENTS:

Two or three beanbags, two decks of cards (for the variation)

PREPARATION:

None

DIRECTIONS:

1. Ask the class to stand in a circle.
2. Call out the name and toss the beanbag to one of the group members.
3. The student who caught the beanbag must explain what he learned in rehearsal or what material was covered in the class.
4. After the first student has finished, he calls out a new name and tosses out the beanbag to that student. Repeat the process.
5. Inform the students that they cannot repeat students until everyone has had a turn. This guarantees 100% participation while you assess the entire class' comprehension of the material covered.
6. Change the question once satisfied with the entire class' understanding.

VARIATIONS:

- Substitute beach balls, soft foam balls, or wadded pieces of paper.
- Throw two or three beanbags and say people's names within a couple of seconds of each other. As names and beanbags are tossed, the game will get crazy. This variation keeps the students on their toes as they have to be ready with their answers.
- **Card Toss** Hand out playing cards each time a student answers a question correctly (or exhibits model behavior) during the rehearsal. At the end of the week see who has the best poker hand. All you need is one or two decks of playing cards.

ICE TIP:

- Information should be caught and not just taught.

PURPOSE:
In addition to strengthening listening skills, the students must be patient with one another. There is physical contact in this icebreaker.

REQUIREMENTS:
One chair for each student (without desktops attached)

PREPARATION:
Consider the list that you will call out

DIRECTIONS:
1. Ask students to move their chairs in a large circle with the chair backs facing the inside of the circle. When the chairs are as tight as possible, students should sit.
2. Tell the class that you will call out a descriptive statement. If the statement applies to the students, they move one seat to their right. If a student doesn't fit the description, she stays seated in his chair. Many people will be moving at the same time.
3. The results after several statements will be students sitting on others' laps.

Ideas for the instructor to call out:
- If you are wearing a shirt with a college logo, move to the right.
- If you have a pet, move to the right.
- If you like coffee more than soda, move to the right.
- If you love algebra, move to the right.
- If you play an instrument, move to the right.
- If you like scary movies, move to the right.
- If you like to scrapbook, move to the right.
- If you made your bed this morning, move to the right.
- If you have been in a hospital this year as a patient or a visitor, move to the right
- If you have all of your music memorized for this class, move to the right.

VARIATION:
A Magical Chair-Breaker Icebreaker The class will be amazed at this advanced variation that requires core strength. Four volunteers sit sideways on four chairs with their knees facing to the right side of the chair. Simultaneously, the volunteers lean back while keeping their feet flat on the floor. Each person's head rests on the stomach of the person to his immediate left. Slowly, pull out each of the four chairs. The result is a pyramid of four people "magically" suspended in the air (their feet are supporting their weight). Carefully slip the chairs back under the volunteers so they can sit up slowly.

ICE TIP:
Be sure the class is focused before trying the *Chair-Breaker* Icebreaker. The chair games require participants capable of mature thinking. If a student is being silly, he could get hurt or harm another student.

I C E B R E A K E R S

partner up, sit down

Energizers – Stress Reducers and Let's Get Physical

PURPOSE:
This icebreaker involves the entire class in a type of musical chairs, without the chairs. When your choir appears to be tired or overanxious, this icebreaker raises heart rates and energy level for the rest of the rehearsal.

REQUIREMENTS:
CD player
Music on a CD (or a live musician)

PREPARATION:
None

DIRECTIONS:
1. Instruct 2/3 of the class to form one large circle facing clockwise. The remaining class members make a smaller circle inside the large circle and face counter-clockwise.
2. Inform the students to start moving in the direction they are facing when they hear music. When the music stops, the students grab the hands of someone in the other circle and quickly sits on the floor. The last students to find partners are eliminated and should referee the rest of the game.
3. Continue the icebreaker until the last pair is declared winners!

VARIATIONS:
- **Movin' In Style** Ask the participants to move their bodies in whatever style of music they hear. For example, the students jog in the circles to fast music, skip to swing music or shuffle-step to a country song. Continue with the instructions above.
- **Partners All Around** For a silly challenge, blindfold the inner circle of students and follow the directions for the rest of the icebreaker. Although more time-consuming, this variation generates twice the laughs.
- **Posing Teams** Encourage creativity by asking students to create poses with other students on their team on the floor that best represent the style of music played.

ICE TIP:
If you have fewer boys than girls in your class, instruct the boys to make the inner circle and the girls to make the outer circle.

ICEBREAKERS

the quest

PURPOSE:
The group must rely on the contents of their backpacks. The more participants involved, the better the odds are to win this icebreaker.

REQUIREMENTS:
Pieces of paper for the team signatures
List of items for *The Quest*

PREPARATION:
Prepare a list that a judge can call out for *The Quest*. Here are some examples:
- An item of clothing featuring a cartoon character
- A person with braces
- A person with painted toenails
- An article of clothing with vertical stripes
- A person blowing a bubble and the bubble must still be in good shape
- A boy wearing lipstick
- A sock with a hole in it (Hint: All socks have holes. It is what you put your foot in)
- Two people wearing the same shoes (Hint: Students trade shoes)
- A picture of an animal (Hint: Look at credit cards or cell phones images)
- Three boys linking arms and doing a can-can dance

DIRECTIONS:
1. Divide the class into teams of five to ten people and distribute to each team one piece of paper for signatures.
2. Ask a volunteer to serve as the judge. The judge decides where the teams can search for items (backpacks, purse, desks, or the classroom) and calls out items by saying, "I am on a quest for _____."
3. Challenge the teams to search for the items that the judge is seeking. When the team finds an item, one person from each team runs to the judge to present it to the judge.
4. Score the groups according to the successful order of appearance. The first team to present the correct item to the judge is awarded 10 points. The second team to successfully present the correct item is awarded 9 points and so on down to one point for the last place group. Non-participating groups score zero points.
5. At the end of the game, add up the points to declare a winner.

VARIATION:
Get creative! Ask the class to brainstorm and name items for future quests.

ICE TIP:
As a safety precaution, the teams should stay at least three feet away from the judge.

I C E B R E A K E R S

pack a bug

Energizers – Stress Reducers and Let's Get Physical

PURPOSE:
This game brings up a bit of nostalgia. Back in the 1970s, it was the craze to squeeze many people into a little Volkswagon Bug®. History and good ideas repeat themselves. Share the fun with your students.

REQUIREMENTS:
Provide one large-sized sheet of poster board (at least 22" x 28") for each 10–12 person group. Size of the board or mat may vary depending on how many people you are stuffing into the "car space." You may use different colored poster boards for each group.

PREPARATION:
None

DIRECTIONS:
1. Explain that the goal is to cram as many members on the piece of poster board without anybody's arms or legs touching the floor. This may be done by people leaning "out the windows" of the pretend car, standing so close that everyone fits on the paper, or stacking the members in various formations.
2. Inform the groups they will need to hold the pose for 15 seconds.

VARIATIONS:
- Use a Twister® mat or masking tape to partition off the required space if poster board is unavailable.
- **Imaginary Telephone Booth** Put limits on the height and width of the participants by perhaps only using people up to six feet tall. The groups will have to be more creative in this variation.
- Platform shoes and leisure suits are optional. ☺

ICE TIPS:
- Safety is an important factor in this game; students must be in complete control at all times.
- Participants need to focus and think through their placement within the group.
- Make every attempt to include everyone in this icebreaker activity. If someone does not want to participate, he can be the photographer or a judge.
- Remember a camera to record the hilarious results (or contact the school photographer for some great shots for the yearbook or newspaper).

ICEBREAKERS

musical parts

Energizers – Stress Reducers and Let's Get Physical

PURPOSE:
Students interact with each other while enjoying music in a non-threatening environment.

REQUIREMENTS:
CD player
CDs (brought by students)

PREPARATION:
Ask students to bring CDs of their favorite music. Students should be aware that if they bring their music, the lyrics must not be offensive or contain inappropriate subject matter.

DIRECTIONS:
1. Ask for a student to volunteer her CD and man the CD player.
2. Instruct the students that when the music begins, they should move in some fashion (dance, walk, job, any other high energy movement). When the music stops, call out a random number and a part of the body (for instance, "Five elbows!" As fast as possible, five students touch their elbows together).
3. Instead of eliminating students, allow the students to continue to play.

VARIATION:
Backpack Find If you prefer to avoid using body parts, try a variation of *Musical Parts* using items found in backpacks (i.e. three math books, five erasers, nine calculators, six contact cases, two pieces of gum, etc.)

ICE TIPS:
- Students enjoy the music, competition, physical movement, and interaction with their classmates.
- Great icebreaker for large groups!
- An icebreaker like this would definitely keep the faculty and administration alert on an in-service day!
- Take notice of the natural leaders who are forming the groups.
- To avoid injuries, call out small numbers with body parts above the shoulders!

I C E B R E A K E R S

ring around the circle

Energizers – Stress Reducers and Let's Get Physical

PURPOSE:
Group members must be patient and cooperate with one another to move two hula-hoops completely around a circle.

REQUIREMENTS:
Two hula-hoops for each circle of students

PREPARATION:
None

DIRECTIONS:
1. Instruct students to stand in a circle and hold hands.
2. Thread one hula-hoop around the hands of two people. They must first let go of hands, and then stick their arms through and lock hands through the ring of the hula hoop.
3. Challenge the participants to avoid breaking their grip while passing a hula-hoop around the circle. To accomplish this, the students must contort and move their bodies to transfer the hula-hoop from one person to the next.
4. Congratulate the entire group when the hula-hoop returns to the starting pair.

VARIATIONS:
- **Two Rings Around the Circle** Activate two hula-hoops at the same time. This is a difficult assignment, but it is possible to achieve. For success, the group members need to discuss a strategy to pass the hula-hoops through each other two different times. One person starts the game and places a hula-hoop on his right arm and a second hula-hoop on his left arm. Let go of hands as you place the hula hoops around your arms and then re-connect hands.
- **Hoop Line Race** Line the students into two rows of equal numbers of participants. Announce that each line will race to move the hula-hoop from the beginning of the line to the end and back again.

ICE TIPS:
- This icebreaker works best for a circle of 10–20 students. If there are more than 20 students, break them into multiple circles.
- As with many of the icebreakers, videotape the activity. Play the footage back for the students after a concert or contest as a reward.

ready, set, throw

PURPOSE:
This wild and crazy icebreaker demonstrates the importance of respect. Experience shows that when everyone in class is talking, little is accomplished. However, when the students are courteous in class and listen to the one giving directions, twice as much is accomplished.

REQUIREMENTS:
One dozen ping-pong balls
One beach ball
Stopwatch

PREPARATION:
None

DIRECTIONS:
1. Ask a volunteer to keep record of the number of times the ping-pong balls and the beach ball hit the floor.
2. Toss out one dozen ping-pong balls. The members have two minutes to throw them to each other (not at each other!) and catch as many of them as possible.
3. At the end of the two minutes, ask everyone to pick up all the ping-pong balls.
4. If students are skilled enough to handle one dozen moving ping-pong balls, continue adding more balls until the situation becomes unmanageable.
5. Next, throw out one large beach ball as you explain the goal is for the students to keep the ball moving by catching and tossing it back in the air.
6. Ask the recorder to report the number of times ping-pong balls hit the floor and how many times the beach ball hit the floor.

VARIATION:
Try this icebreaker with one dozen balloons.

ICE TIPS:
- Lead a discussion that allows students to give feedback about their observations of this activity. Stress how little can be accomplished when so much is happening at the same time (represented by the flying ping-pong balls) compared to when there is just one center of focus (represented by the single beach ball).
- Most people achieve more success when they focus on one thing at a time. While some people try to live their lives in a flurry of multi-tasking activities, the vast majority of students learn and retain the most when distractions are minimized and they can focus on one subject or person (teacher) at a time.

ICEBREAKERS

eyes shut – now move!

Energizers – Stress Reducers and Let's Get Physical

PURPOSE:

Eyes Shut – Now Move! forces students to listen and follow directions. Body awareness and spatial memory are important concepts explored as students attempt to hold poses and move as instructed.

REQUIREMENTS:

None

PREPARATION:

None

DIRECTIONS:

1. Inform the students they will carry out a series of instructions of specific body movements without looking at their own bodies or the leader.
2. Instruct the students to stand and close their eyes.
3. Read up to 10 statements that the students must act out.

   Examples of body movements:
   - Sit on the floor with your legs in front of you.
   - Turn your head to the right.
   - Stretch your left hand up to the ceiling.
   - Cross your ankles, placing the right foot over the left.
   - Bend your left arm, resting it on your head.

4. Tell the students to freeze in the final position and open their eyes to look around the room at their peers.
5. Ask them to compare their final body placement with their neighbors' position. Do they match? If not, why?

VARIATION:

Try variations with very specific directions or very general suggestions. Imagine the different results when students hear, "Place your right arm out horizontally and bend your elbow in a 45-degree angle so your fingers are facing up," versus statements like, "Move your right arm to the side of your body," or "Rotate your body and freeze." Enjoy the personality of the poses and the various choices made by the participants.

ICE TIP:

This icebreaker game is a reminder that we are all created differently. Each person thinks and moves independently. This is also a good icebreaker to reinforce body awareness and balance.

ICEBREAKERS

fact or fiction

Problem Solving – Achieving Group Goals

PURPOSE:

This icebreaker encourages students to get to know and appreciate each other, while discovering common ground, unique interests and experiences.

REQUIREMENTS:

A writing board
Markers

PREPARATION:

None

DIRECTIONS:

1. Inform the students that each will take a turn to write two statements, one fact and one fiction, on the board. To gain insight, the class members can either ask questions with "yes" or "no" answers or vote without any discussion as to how well they know their classmate. The class votes (by a show of hands or simple ballot form) which statement is fact and which statement is fiction.

2. Once the students have reached a consensus, allow the student who authored the statements to identify which is fictitious and which is factual. This is a good time for the student to share background information about the factual statement.

VARIATIONS:

- Try an electronic variation of *Fact or Fiction* where the students e-mail their statements. This variation adds a new dimension when the class cannot see a player's face.
- As a writing icebreaker assignment, ask the student to write out the fact and fiction statements. Carefully choose several of the examples to present to the class, writing the fact and fiction statements under the student's name on the board. Repeat the process.

ICE TIPS:

- *Fact or Fiction* works well with groups who are just getting to know each other. Students can instinctively pick up nuances between fact and fiction when provided with very little information.
- *Fact or Fiction* also works well with students who have known each other for a long time. Students might learn a thing or two about their friends that they think they know well.

p.b. and j. sandwich recipe

Problem Solving – Achieving Group Goals

PURPOSE:
Problem solving provides opportunities for cooperation in small and large groups.

REQUIREMENTS:
Note cards, writing utensils, jars of peanut butter and jelly, a loaf of bread, knife paper plates, paper towels

PREPARATION:
Discuss the objective of the icebreaker with the pre-chosen listener.

DIRECTIONS:
1. Without discussion, instruct students to write a recipe for a peanut butter and jelly sandwich on a note card.
2. Collect the recipes and randomly select one of them from the stack.
3. Ask the pre-chosen listener to come to the front of the class and ask for a volunteer to read the recipe aloud. They should stand back-to-back so they cannot see each other's actions.
4. The listener should carry out each action very literally. For example, if the recipe says to put the peanut butter on the bread, the listener sets the jar of peanut butter on the loaf of bread. If the recipe states to put the knife in the peanut butter, the listener should stick the knife through the jar (the recipe did not say open the jar first). If the instruction is to scoop jelly on the bread, the listener should scoop jelly out of the jar using his hand (the recipe did not mention using a spoon).
5. At the end of the activity, ask the students if anyone wants to eat the sandwich. Quite often, this activity will produce a mess and a good laugh for your class.
6. In conclusion, lead a discussion about the results of poorly written directions that are not thorough. The outcome may be an ugly mess and sometimes paper towels are not available for clean up!

VARIATION:
Pair students to read recipes and build sandwiches with the given instructions.

ICE TIPS:
- For this icebreaker to have the most impact, the chosen recipe should be basic and not descriptive.
- This is a good exercise to observe who can communicate and who can listen to details. A lack of communication can be the source of conflict in an ensemble.

take note!

PURPOSE:

This decision-making icebreaker provides the class with the opportunity to communicate and solve a problem together. Train your students to pick up on even the smallest of details.

REQUIREMENTS:

None

PREPARATION:

None

DIRECTIONS:

1. Divide the class into pairs (try using another icebreaker to pair up the class. For example, instruct students to find a partner with the same color of eyes).
2. Ask the pairs to sit, facing each other.
3. Allow 90 seconds for each couple to discuss subjects with which they feel passionately (perhaps provide topics for discussion). Practicing good listening habits, the students should focus 100% on each other to observe all details about their partner.
4. Ask the partners to turn around and secretly to change three things about their appearance (i.e. rolling up sleeves, buttoning up, turn belt backwards, etc.).
5. Direct students to turn and face their partner to assess what has been changed.
6. Praise the teams who have paid the most attention to details.

VARIATIONS:

- **MUSICAL TAKE NOTE!** Try a listening variation by using a piece of music that your choir is currently preparing, reinforcing musical concepts and refining the listening skills of the choir members. Divide the choir in half. The first half performs the piece while the other half listens intently. Next, discuss three details in the score that you want the performers to improve. Repeat the performance. The listening half of the choir will share the audible changes that they heard. Offer clues if no one volunteers any changes that were made. Direct the first half to sing again.

- **Teacher Takes Note** The teacher steps out of the room for 45 seconds. Three students change their appearance. How observant is the teacher? Students will love this variation.

ICE TIP:

Discuss the following quote... "Countless, unseen details are often the only difference between mediocre and magnificent."

ICEBREAKERS

bring a "t" to the circle

Problem Solving – Achieving Group Goals

PURPOSE:
This exercise is an excellent "getting-to-know-you" game encouraging the participants to bond quickly. It also builds non-verbal communication skills.

REQUIREMENTS:
T-shirts
Box or laundry basket

PREPARATION:
Inform students to bring a t-shirt on a specified date that reflects the student's personality (with a picture, logo, color, etc.). Ask them to keep their t-shirt hidden in a sack or book bag, hiding it from their peers.

DIRECTIONS:
1. As the students arrive, ask them to drop their t-shirts from home in a box or basket and to sit in a large circle.
2. Pass the basket and ask the students to select one shirt that is not theirs.
3. Tell them to examine the t-shirt attributes (not the size) and determine to whom the shirt belongs. The students should move around the room to give the shirt to the person that they suspect is the owner and then return to their seat. Note: All students must end up with a shirt and each person can receive only one shirt.
4. Going around the circle, ask the class to vote by a show of hands if they agree that each shirt was presented to the correct owner. Each student can either confirm or deny the match.
5. Allow each student to explain why he chose that special shirt to bring to the activity and how it represents his personality.

VARIATIONS:
- **Bring "U" to the Circle** Try this activity bringing something <u>you</u> love. Variations of this icebreaker are endless. Try the activity using baby pictures, writing utensils, stuffed animals, bookmarks, favorite books, favorite quotes.
- Students enjoy when the teacher also participates by bringing a personal item.

ICE TIPS:
- Make sure your students are comfortable revealing personal information.
- Be sure no one is left out; the accompanist, room moms, and booster president can all join in this fun.

I C E B R E A K E R S

singo

PURPOSE:

People like to play bingo! *Singo* stimulates interaction between performers and allows students to shine. Participants are more willing to share talents and information in a non-threatening environment.

REQUIREMENTS:

Note cards or sticky notes
Writing utensil

PREPARATION:

Ask students to write an interesting or secret fact about themselves. Collect these facts to create bingo cards with the number of squares on the grid directly corresponding to the number of students in the group.

DIRECTIONS:

1. Form teams of two to four members.
2. Pass out the *Singo* card to each student.
3. Give the teams an opportunity to mingle with other small groups. The goal is for the students to fill in the *Singo* card grid by getting autographs from the people who most identify with the facts. When a team successfully fills in every grid on their cards, they yell, "*Singo*!"
4. Allow each student whose fact is highlighted to respond.

VARIATION:

First Impressions Grid Introduce a variation with very general questions. Prior to class, compose a list of descriptive first impression statements. The students' goal is to fill in the grid with the names of students who satisfy the first impression. For example, the statement to be completed could be, "_____ is an animal lover." If a student is approached and the answer is "yes," he will sign his name on the grid. If the answer is "no," encourage more interactions between the students to find another first impression.

Here are a few examples for First Impressions Grid:

- _____enjoys '80s music
- _____loves thriller movies
- _____values time with friends
- _____works out at a gym
- _____eats gourmet meals

ICE TIP:

If there are too many facts to create a grid, create different grids for each age level, each section, or for smaller groups of students. A prize for the winning team can be motivating. Candy awards work well, but consider inexpensive, yet rewarding prizes like letting the winning team assign who will put away music folders or chairs after a rehearsal.

icebergs

Problem Solving – Achieving Group Goals

PURPOSE:

Icebergs challenges students to follow simple directions. Teamwork is imperative if the group strives to achieve its goal. *Icebergs* game clears the way for learning.

REQUIREMENTS:

White paper (one piece for each student plus one additional piece)

PREPARATION:

Place the pieces of paper (representing icebergs) in a straight line about 15 inches apart on the floor.

DIRECTIONS:

1. Divide the class into two teams.

2. Explain each piece of paper represents an iceberg and the floor represents the freezing water. The challenge is for students to move from iceberg to iceberg without falling into the freezing water.

3. Share the following "Ice Tips" with the students before starting the game:

   - Only one person may touch or stand on an iceberg at a time.
   - Students may move in either direction when trying to get to a neighboring iceberg, but no part of their body can touch the water.
   - Students can help each other move and maintain their balance (students can touch an empty iceberg if trying to maintain balance).
   - The icebergs cannot be moved during the game.
   - Clothing and shoes are a part of the person and cannot be removed or dropped during the game. If a shoe falls off or a sweater slips off, the student "freezes to death" and loses points.
   - Students may lift another student off an occupied iceberg and can step on the feet of teammates.
   - If any of the above rules are broken, the entire group must start over from the beginning.

4. Ask the students to choose an iceberg to stand on, leaving the extra iceberg at one end of the line open.

5. Start the game.

6. At the conclusion, the students should be in the reverse order that they started the game.

VARIATIONS:

- This icebreaker works best with five to twenty students.
- If you have a big group, use several lines of icebergs with multiple teams to compete for the best time.

ICE TIP:

Keep in mind that the more people that are involved, the tougher the task.

ICEBREAKERS

knot twister

PURPOSE:
This icebreaker engages the students fully and encourages competition.

REQUIREMENTS:
25-100 foot extension cord (for the variation)

PREPARATION:
None

DIRECTIONS:
1. Divide students into teams of eight to sixteen people (logical groups could be music sections or men vs. women).
2. Ask the teams to form a circle with all of the participants' shoulders touching.
3. Instruct the members of each group to reach into the circle to grab the hands of two other people (not the people directly to either side).
4. Challenge the students to untangle themselves without releasing their hands. This is a physical activity where participants step over hands, back track, or twist hands around to solve the puzzle.
5. Observe the activity as the students work together towards the end goal of standing shoulder-to-shoulder with the people whose hands they are now holding.

VARIATIONS:
- **Human Slip Knot** Students form a single file line. The first person leans over and puts his right hand through his legs and takes hold of the left hand of the person directly behind him. The second person (still holding the right hand of the person in front of him with his left hand) puts his right hand through his legs to take the left hand of the person directly behind him. Continue until everyone is leaning over and is holding hands with the people in front and directly behind. The person at the end of the line lies on his back. The person in front of him carefully walks backwards over the person lying down, still holding hands. The rest of the line gingerly walks backward as each person lies on his back without releasing the hands of the people in front or behind each individual.
- **Extension Cord Untwist** The goal of this icebreaker is for students to untangle the cord without removing their grip from the cord. Knot an extension cord several times before the game begins. Ask each person to grab a section of the cord with his right hand. Students may use their left hand to help untangle the cord. Unknotting an extension cord is a handy skill!

ICE TIP:
This icebreaker may seem impossible but it will work! This activity is a good lesson that patience is a virtue. Welcome creative thinking among the group to solve the puzzle.

ICEBREAKERS

circle of trust

Trust Building – Establishing Leadership

PURPOSE:
This objective is to inspire trust among the group and to discover how each individual contributes to the balance in the circle.

REQUIREMENTS:
None

PREPARATION:
None

DIRECTIONS:
1. Instruct the students to move into one large circle with every other person facing out and the next person facing into the middle of the circle.
2. Each participant grips the wrists of the people to his right and left.
3. Instruct the students to simultaneously and slowly lean into the direction they are facing.
4. Challenge the students to lean even further. If the circle remains strong and connected, the core of the group should support itself.

VARIATION:
Sitting Circle of Trust Stand in a tight circle and everyone faces to the right. Each student places his hands on the shoulders of the person directly in front of him. On the count of three, everyone in the circle slowly bends their knees and moves to a sitting position. If the seated circle is stable, ask students to raise both arms high in the air. If successful, the students will sit on each other's laps and the strength of the team will support the circle.

ICE TIPS:
Discussions could include:
- Everyone should be involved and connected in the circle.
- What happens in an ensemble or a team when someone does not pull his own weight and support the group goals?
- What happens when people do not listen to a leader?
- Why should the ensemble support their peers in and out of the rehearsal?

ICEBREAKERS

trust walk

Trust Building – Establishing Leadership

PURPOSE:
Your ensemble will be much stronger when the members trust and depend on each other. Trust builds loyalty.

REQUIREMENTS:
Blindfolds
Obstacle Course
Small and silly toys (for the variation)
(soft foam balls, balloons, rubber insects, stuffed animals, squeaky toys)

PREPARATION:
Determine a route for a safe obstacle course.

DIRECTIONS:
1. Split the students into pairs and designate the older student as the leader.
2. Place the blindfold over the eyes of the younger student.
3. Explain that the leader will talk the blindfolded trusting student through an obstacle course.
4. After the younger blindfolded student has completed the course, ask the pair to switch roles so the older student is now blindfolded and will be talked through the course by the younger student.

VARIATION:
Caterpillar Game This icebreaker variation is virtually the same as the above except students form a line and hold onto the waist of the person in front of them. Only the first person in the line is allowed to see. The caterpillar leader must navigate the rest of the body around the room and through obstacles. The leader can have the caterpillar climb over, crawl under, and go around objects.

ICE TIPS:
• This exercise is fun to do outside but it is important to consider the terrain. Provide a smooth path so students won't trip.
• Some students do not like to be blindfolded. If this is of concern, trust them to participate by shutting their eyes.

true treasure hunt

Trust Building – Establishing Leadership

PURPOSE:
True Treasure Hunt is a great way to express gratitude to the people that help students use their talents daily. Acknowledge the people who are "treasures" in your own school.

REQUIREMENTS:
Stationery
List of items for the treasure/scavenger hunt (for the variation)

PREPARATION:
- Choose the individuals to thank on the *True Treasure Hunt*.
- Create specialized stationery on departmental letterhead by adding a header, THANK YOU FOR ALL YOU DO! on each sheet of paper.
- Notify administration and staff in advance that students may be stopping by their room or office and ask them to send back some sort of proof that the mission was accomplished.

DIRECTIONS:
1. Explain that a *True Treasure Hunt* gives the students an opportunity to show staff, teachers, and administrators their appreciation by creating a note of gratitude.
2. Break the students into groups of four to eight people.
3. Allow time for groups to write personal messages to the "treasured" people.
4. Deliver the messages to the True Treasures. If they are aware of the impending visits, ask them to send back a colored paper clip to prove the mission was accomplished.

Listed below are ideas of people for *True Treasure Hunt*:
- School secretary
- Custodian
- Cafeteria staff
- Coach or coaches
- Librarian (this also ensures the kids know the location of the library!)
- Accompanist (leave a note on the piano bench)
- Student teacher
- A favorite teacher
- Principal (this should be a positive visitation for the student)

VARIATION:
Statistical Treasure Hunt Provide a handout for a treasure hunt (for examples, see page 48) and ask the students to answer the questions. After five minutes, add the points.

ICE TIP:
A simple thank you or pat on the back can boost the morale of overlooked and underappreciated support staff and administrators.

ICEBREAKERS

_____Musical Instruments	One point for each instrument the group members play
_____Shoe Sizes	Total the shoe sizes of the group (round half sizes up)
_____Dominant Hands	One point for each right-handed member
	Three points for each left-handed member
	Five points for each ambidextrous member
_____Pets	One point for each pet owned by the group members
_____Hospital Visits	One point for each stay in a hospital in the past year
	Five points for visiting someone in the hospital
_____Vision	One point if you are wearing contact lenses
	Two points if you are wearing glasses
	Subtract five points if you are wearing sunglasses
_____Concerts	One point for each concert attended in the past month
_____Homework	Five points if you have completed today's homework
	Three points if you will take homework home
	Zero points if you are unsure of your assignments
_____Socks	One point for black socks
	Two points for white socks
	Three points for colored socks or tights
	Zero points for no socks
_____Family Size	One point for each family member of the group members
_____Breakfast	Three points for eating a healthy breakfast
	Two points for eating anything for breakfast
	Zero points if you skipped breakfast
_____School Spirit	Five points for each clothing item featuring your school logo
	Three points for school colors
_____Belts	Three points for a brown belt
	Two points for a black belt
	One point for any other color belt
	Zero points for no belt
_____Music Group	Ten points for every musical activity members participate in
_____Attendance	Ten points for perfect attendance in this class
_____	TOTAL GROUP SCORE

listening game

Trust Building – Establishing Leadership

PURPOSE:
Improve listening skills by hearing with one's eyes, ears, and heart.

REQUIREMENTS:
Stopwatch

PREPARATION:
None

DIRECTIONS:
1. Divide the group into pairs. Ask students to sit next to someone they have not spoken with this week.
2. Designate the person with the cleanest shoes as the talker and the other person is the listener.
3. Instruct the talkers to speak about something that makes them happy. Do not let the talkers know that the listeners will not be listening. Privately, instruct the listeners not to pay any attention to the talkers. The listener should sit with the talker but should be unresponsive. The talkers have 60 seconds to try to converse with the listeners.
4. Stop the conversations and give new directions. This time give the talkers 60 seconds to speak about a topic that makes them angry. Instruct the listeners to ignore the talkers or pretend that their subjects are silly.
5. Stop the talker's dialogue and encourage the pair to reflect on how having a one-way dialogue made the talker feel.
6. Try the game once more, only this time let the talkers speak about something they are passionate about and for this last round, ask the listeners to be truly attentive.
7. Stop after 60 seconds and discuss the talker's thoughts on this exercise. If time, switch and let the listeners see how it feels to carry on a one-way conversation with apathetic partners. Discuss how it felt when a person was not really listening.

VARIATION:
Instruct the class to listen to two selections of music. Give students a writing assignment to complete while they are supposed to be listening to the music. Play the music a second time and ask the students to listen attentively using all of their senses. Which time was the easiest to listen to the music? Did they have trouble staying alert or focusing either time?

ICE TIPS:
- Every human has two ears, two eyes, and one mouth. The successful people in life are those that know how to use their senses in the correct proportion.
- Discuss how listening determines our leadership capabilities. When listening, are you using eye contact, body language, and facial gestures?
- More success will be achieved in school (and in life) if and when one learns to truly listen.

I C E B R E A K E R S

100 headliner questions

Trust Building – Establishing Leadership

PURPOSE:
This series of questions teaches respect and discipline as students must quietly wait their turn to speak and to avoid interruptions. In addition, this icebreaker also heightens students' listening skills.

REQUIREMENTS:
Time for questions and answers (Sample questions provided on pages 51-52)

PREPARATION:
Determine which questions from the list work best for each class.

DIRECTIONS:
1) The instructor reads a question from the list and students take turns answering the question honestly.
2) Begin with simple non-threatening questions (name a favorite movie or TV show) and eventually advance to more involved and probing questions (share an embarrassing moment or who do you emulate as a performer or as a person?).

There are three simple rules in the *Headliner Question* icebreaker:
- Students must listen to and respect the person talking.
- While the speaker has the floor, no one else talks or interrupts.
- The information shared is private and confidential. What is said in rehearsal, stays in the rehearsal.

VARIATIONS:
- If your group is on tour, turn this icebreaker into a travel game. If the ensemble is split between vehicles, ask students to speculate how fellow classmates would answer the questions. When arriving at the destination, quiz the classmates to measure how closely the correct answers are to those that were speculated.
- Empower the students to add their own questions to the list. Chances are they will enjoy composing questions as much as answering them.

ICE TIPS:
- Students feel ownership when they disclose information about themselves.
- The 100 Headliner questions is a series of questions. I use these with my select showchoir, the Butler Headliners. I hope they will make as big of an impact in your classroom as they have in mine.
- This icebreaker is a favorite activity of all ages. Of course, answers will differ between elementary children, high school and college students and church choir members! Regardless of age, place, or purpose, almost everyone enjoys answering the questions and hearing the responses.
- If questions are personal or emotional, give the participants the option of passing their turn or sharing at a later time. People need to feel comfortable in their level of involvement.

100 headliner questions

(cont'd page 52)

Compiled by Valerie Lippoldt Mack and dedicated to the Butler Headliners

1. Where were you born? (Name of the hospital, town, state, room)
2. Describe your first home.
3. As a child, what gave you comfort? (person, pet, stuffed animal, pillow, blanket)
4. What is the greatest joy in your life?
5. What is your greatest fear?
6. What is the last book you read?
7. What is your favorite color and why?
8. What scares you the most in life?
9. What is your biggest sorrow up to this point in your life? If situational, can it be repaired?
10. Describe the greatest musical experience of your life.
11. Who inspires you and why?
12. Who is the most honest person you know?
13. Describe your most embarrassing moment. (the G-rated two minute version)
14. For what are you most thankful?
15. For whom are you most thankful?
16. What was the most memorable Christmas gift you have received?
17. What was the most memorable Christmas gift you have given?
18. Name a New Year's resolution that you were able to keep.
19. What was your first pet's name?
20. What is your favorite subject in school? What is your favorite subject in life?
21. What is your favorite restaurant and menu item?
22. What is your favorite fast food?
23. What is your favorite movie and why?
24. What is your favorite movie concession?
25. Describe your most memorable birthday celebration.
26. What kind of birthday cake would you request?
27. What are your hobbies?
28. What is a hobby for which you wish you had time or talent?
29. What is a secret about yourself that nobody knows?
30. What is the best quality to have in a girlfriend, boyfriend, or a spouse?
31. Describe your perfect date. (without listing names)
32. What is your favorite Christmas carol?
33. Where do you see yourself one year from now?
34. Where do you see yourself five years from now?
35. Where do you see yourself ten years from now?
36. If you could be an animal, which kind would you choose?
37. What insect would you like to see become extinct?
38. Which movie star are you like the most?
39. If you were casting a movie, who would you cast to play yourself?
40. If you were casting a movie, who would you choose to be your co-star?
41. What is your favorite line from a movie?
42. What celebrity do you find most irritating?
43. What is the funniest movie you have ever seen?
44. What is the scariest movie you have ever seen?
45. What is your favorite "feel good" movie of all time?
46. If you could change one thing about your personality, what would that be?
47. Name what makes you most passionate.
48. If you received $100 ($1,000, $100,000, etc.), how would you spend it?
49. What is your favorite activity on weekends?
50. Describe your perfect vacation. Where would you go and would you be alone or with others?

ICEBREAKERS

100 headliner questions

Compiled by Valerie Lippoldt Mack

51. What is your favorite book? (or substitute TV sitcom, TV commercial, month, fashion, etc.)
52. What is your favorite clothing store?
53. What is your proudest moment?
54. Describe your most embarrassing hairstyle.
55. What was the destination of your longest car trip?
56. Have you ever experienced miracles in your life?
57. What would you like carved on your tombstone?
58. What talents and skills do you desire?
59. What are advantages of being tall or short?
60. What do people compliment you on the most?
61. What is it about you that people find irresistible?
62. What kind of parent will you be?
63. What kind of grandparent will you be?
64. What makes you most angry?
65. What is your biggest pet peeve?
66. What is the best purchase you have made in your lifetime?
67. What is the worst purchase you have made in your lifetime?
68. What latest trend surprises you?
69. If you were able to enjoy the finer things in life, how would you treat yourself?
70. When was the last time you giggled?
71. What do you do for exercise?
72. What is your least favorite form of exercise?
73. What is your favorite clean joke? (You must tell it to the class!)
74. What is the best advice you have ever received?
75. As a child, what was your favorite book?
76. If you were a teacher, what subject would you teach?
77. What is your best Halloween costume? What is your most embarrassing Halloween costume?
78. What word best describes your computer knowledge?
79. What technological breakthrough do you think will revolutionize your generation?
80. If you could add any word to the dictionary, what word would you add?
81. What is the most beautiful word in the English language?
82. If you were snowbound for an entire week, what three items would you want near you?
83. What do you consider is the greatest dessert of all time?
84. If you could be a member of a TV sitcom family, which family would you choose?
85. What are your two favorite television stations?
86. What commercial product do you refuse to endorse and why?
87. What object from home are you most embarrassed to own?
88. What is your lifelong dream?
89. What is your greatest phobia?
90. What question would you ask the President of the United States of America?
91. What is the toughest occupation in the world?
92. If you had a blank canvas and a paintbrush, what would you paint?
93. If you could be a famous actor, writer, athlete, dancer, or musician, which would you choose?
94. List one word that describes how you dance.
95. Have you had your fifteen minutes of fame? When, what, where, and why?
96. What question do you have for the teacher?
97. What are your top ten characteristics of a best friend?
98. What song reminds you of a past or present relationship?
99. Describe your childhood dream. Did you reach your goal?
100. What life lessons will you leave? What is your legacy?

ICEBREAKERS

high point share

Trust Building – Establishing Leadership

PURPOSE:
Sometimes students are not given an opportunity to share exciting news about good things happening in their lives. *High Point Share* takes just a few minutes of classroom time, but provides a wonderful boost in the attitude of group members while compelling others to feel good about themselves in and out of the classroom.

REQUIREMENTS:
None

PREPARATION:
None

DIRECTIONS:
1. Invite a volunteer to stand and share the best thing of the day or the week.
2. If time allows, allow each person to talk about the greatest thing that happened that day or week.
3. If students are reluctant to share, ask volunteers to share the best thing that happened to them throughout the semester, a holiday break, spring break, the summer, on stage, etc.

VARIATION:
Discuss the following statements:
- The best thing about being in this group is...
- The best thing that happened in rehearsal today was...
- The best thing that has ever happened to me musically was...
- I am excited for the next performance because...
- My favorite musical selection of all time is...

ICE TIPS:
- Introduce this icebreaker at least once a semester with each class. Amazing energy and positive vibes are generated from this simple exercise. This icebreaker works well with all ages of people, students, church choir, fellow faculty, and even family members around the dinner table.
- Unless a student is emotionally connected to the class and to the instructor, he will lack the motivation to learn.

ICEBREAKERS

group goals

Goal Setting – Developing Group Dynamics

PURPOSE:

Although you may have ideas who are the strongest leaders in your classes, this icebreaker will draw out leaders in smaller groups. The extra bonus is individuals realize that they must be able to communicate in any size group.

REQUIREMENTS:

Notebook paper

Blank poster boards or chalkboard

Markers or chalk

PREPARATION:

None

DIRECTIONS:

1. Split the class into groups of four members.
2. Explain the directions for *Group Goals*
   - Each group creates a list of the top ten goals for the ensemble.
   - The group prioritizes the goals from one to ten, with one being the most important goal and ten being the least important goal. They should list them in the determined order on a poster board, chalkboard, or a piece of paper.
   - Pair two groups to work together to repeat the process (although the group is larger, the same instructions apply).
   - Continue pairing the groups until all teams are working together as one large group to determine the entire class' top ten goals.
   - Challenge the class to reduce those ten goals to the top five goals, creating a dynamic where students work together to rate the goals.
3. List the class' top five collective goals on a poster board to permanently display. It will be a daily reminder of what the class decided their goals are for the year.

VARIATIONS:

- **Movie Time** If you would like to reward your students with a movie day, use the same democratic process to choose a movie title. Students are less likely to complain if the entire class voted on the final decision. Note: Reinforce any rules regarding movie ratings or subject matter before the students nominate and vote.
- This icebreaker, *Group Goals*, can be used to fairly determine any number of important decision-making verdicts that need to be addressed by the class members.

ICE TIPS:

- Although they may not agree during the discussion and voting process, students must work together to compose this list.
- Save this icebreaker for a retreat, a day after a performance, or a day when your choir needs vocal rest. This activity will give the students a break from the normal routine while changing their thought process about the goals of the ensemble.

I C E B R E A K E R S

aluminum foil sculptures

Goal Setting – Developing Group Dynamics

PURPOSE:
Students create an aluminum foil sculpture that is symbolic of their musical and personal goals. Individuals share their goals with the rest of the group.

REQUIREMENTS:
One 20" x 20" sheet of aluminum foil for each participant

PREPARATION:
Prepare the sheets of aluminum foil.

DIRECTIONS:
1. Give the instruction for Aluminum Foil Sculptures
   - The students will mold the aluminum foil into a shape that represents their musical or personal goals for the year. Do not limit the time students have to work on their sculptures.
   - One by one, each student stands and gives an explanation about the goals represented in his musical or personal sculpture.
2. After the show-and-tell presentation, collect each piece to display in the classroom as an arrangement on a table or a drop down array from the ceiling.
3. Save the artwork to give back to the student who achieves the goal!

VARIATION:
If aluminum foil is not available, create the same experience by using gum wrappers for a micro-version of this icebreaker. Other mediums that could be used are toilet paper, wrapping paper, children's building blocks, marshmallows, and toothpicks.

ICE TIPS:
- Make this a voluntary activity. If a student is not comfortable verbalizing the choices she made in creating her piece of art, ask if it can be displayed in the classroom so others can guess the symbolism.
- Students should not be concerned about creating a perfect piece of artwork, rather, encourage them to put thought into what the object should symbolize and what it has to do with the goals for the group.
- *Aluminum Foil Sculptures* is a wonderful way to end a retreat, especially when students are sitting around a campfire.
- Save the foil sculptures and display as ornaments on a tree.

personality quiz

Goal Setting – Developing Group Dynamics

PURPOSE:
This icebreaker allows the ensemble members to discover the similarities and differences of the many personalities within the group.

REQUIREMENTS:
Four poster boards
Personality quiz

PREPARATION:
Prepare one of the different personality quizzes on the four poster boards (see below for a few that are available). Each poster board will feature just one symbol or word. Determine which personality quiz to use for each class and tape the posters on the four walls of the classroom.

DIRECTIONS:
1. Instruct students to sit in front of the poster they find most appealing or gives them comfort.
2. Once everyone has selected a poster, inform the students they have just taken a personality quiz and read aloud the key to the symbols they chose.
3. Allow the participants to discuss the quiz results to determine if the symbols they chose do match their personalities.

VARIATIONS: *(SAMPLE AND ABBREVIATED PERSONALITY QUIZZES ARE LISTED BELOW)*
Shapes Quiz
- ■   Stable and secure
- ●   Loving and caring
- ▲   Intellectual and wise
- Z   Creative, wild, and crazy

Colors Quiz

Blue	Sensitive, social, compassionate and harmonious, non-competitive
Green	Curious, knowledgeable, calm, collected, problem-solver, creative
Gold	Responsible, trustworthy, dependable, punctual, organizer
Orange	Adventuresome, outgoing, spontaneous, charming, fun

Birth Order Quiz

First born/only child	Conscientious, studious, outgoing, leader, respectful, loyal
Second child	Easygoing, gregarious, open-minded, adventurous
Middle child	Free-spirited, friendly, secretive, negotiator
Third born	Social, funny, practical, peace-loving, future-oriented

ICE TIPS:
- If students are commonly assigned tasks in rehearsals, the personality assessments will assist in matching the students to the right jobs.
- As teachers, we must appreciate and understand the differences in our students.
- Contact your local librarian, school counselor, or the internet for more information on personality quizzes.

ICEBREAKERS

topics that matter to me

Goal Setting – Developing Group Dynamics

PURPOSE:
Your class can communicate more effectively when discussions are allowed about important topics and personal beliefs. The objective of this icebreaker is to allow for a time of reflection, to encourage students to understand themselves, and to recognize what is important to each of them.

REQUIREMENTS:
Writing Utensil
Topics That Matter to Me worksheet (see below for sample questions)

PREPARATION:
Prepare the worksheet with questions for *Topics That Matter to Me*

DIRECTIONS:
1. Instruct the students to read the questions on their worksheet and individually fill in the answers. Encourage them to answer the questions honestly and to reflect on their answers to recognize what is important to each of them. This is an activity that builds self-awareness. A person must fully know himself before he can completely share with others. Since this is a very personal assignment, allow enough time without the pressure of time restraints.
2. If the group feels comfortable sharing their answers, form small groups for discussion.

> **Sample questions for *Topics That Matter to Me*:**
> - A goal that is important to me is …
> - One of my personality qualities that I am proud of is …
> - A special memory that stands out is …
> - A person who supports me is …
> - A challenge before me is …
> - I am afraid of …
> - My mentor is …
> - Someone who looks up to me is …
> - I am happiest when I …

VARIATIONS:
- Invite students to invent questions and topics that matter most to them.
- Take the quiz yourself, honestly completing the answers to fully appreciate the risk students are taking by writing their personal beliefs and thoughts.

ICE TIPS:
- Teachers can gain greater knowledge about each student that is necessary to serve the needs of the individuals in the group.
- To change the conversation, change who is participating in the conversation. New voices mean new perspectives. Keep widening the circle.

I C E B R E A K E R S

three life-changers

Goal Setting – Developing Group Dynamics

PURPOSE:

This icebreaker gives the class a chance to reflect on those people that have made an impact on their lives and extend their appreciation to those mentors. This exercise works well at a retreat or around a campfire.

REQUIREMENTS:

Writing utensil
Stationery (for the variation)

PREPARATION:

None

DIRECTIONS:

1. Instruct students to sit in one large circle.
2. Ask students to think of three mentors that have helped them in life.
3. Going around the circle, each student should state the mentors' names and the reasons why each mentor had such an influence and impact on the student's life.
4. Give the class a chance to reflect on the following:
   • Are you proud of the legacy that you are leaving?
   • Will your name be mentioned in the future in a similar circle?
   • How can you change someone's life for the better?
   • With every accomplishment, someone is there, supporting you.

VARIATION:

Three Life-Changer Thank You Notes Supply stationery so students can write their gratitude to their mentors and supporters. More often than not, these people have no idea of the impact they have made in another person's life. When the mentors receive the thank you note, they share in the success and realize their responsibility for the changes in a young person's life. This icebreaker is another way to maintain peer or booster relationships in the community that are beneficial to your program.

ICE TIPS:

• Everyone present should participate, including the instructor, accompanist, and the student teacher. It is advantageous for students to recognize that teachers are human and while they inspired students, they also have mentors who have inspired them.
• Write a thank you note to the people in your life who have made a difference and inspired you!

express yourself

Goal Setting – Developing Group Dynamics

PURPOSE:
Performing groups are stronger when the members trust and support each other. This icebreaker allows students to express themselves, developing relationships with their classmates while using their creative talents.

REQUIREMENTS:
Hat or container

PREPARATION:
Prepare slips of paper with a concept or action written on each.
The students draw a slip of paper with a concept or task each group will aurally or physically demonstrate.

DIRECTIONS:
1. Divide the participants into groups of four to six people.
2. Ask a volunteer from each group to draw one slip of paper and read aloud the statement that they must act out, draw, etc. They can also create a game or compose a song that will convey the message of their concept.
3. Give the group five minutes to discuss and practice their presentation.
4. Allow each group to present.

Concepts/questions for *Express Yourself* icebreaker
- What is a "perfect" rehearsal compared to a "not so perfect" rehearsal?
- Why is respect in the classroom critical?
- Who is the most important person in the room (director, the singers, accompaniment, stage manager, sound person, audience)?
- Demonstrate support for the arts.
- Why is discipline essential?
- Is talent or heart more important to this group?
- Why rehearse music that is challenging?
- What would this group be like if everyone was the same?
- What is the primary goal for this choir?
- What is the choir's reputation around the school? The community?

VARIATION:
Express Yourself in the "Write" Way A more personal writing assignment gives insight to each child's personality, attitude, goals, and opinions.

ICE TIP:
The sky is the limit with this game as students gain a new perspective as they work in a positive and controlled environment.

I C E B R E A K E R S

dynamic poetry

Goal Setting – Developing Group Dynamics

PURPOSE:

Students of any age can create a collaborative poem with the *Dynamic Poetry* activity. Instructors can use this icebreaker to eliminate cliques in the classroom and instead form random student groupings.

REQUIREMENTS:

Paper

Chalkboard, poster board, or dry erase board

Writing Utensils

PREPARATION:

Post the directions on chalkboard, poster board, or dry erase board.

DIRECTIONS:

1. Inform the students work privately to make a list with one noun, one adjective, one adverb, and one preposition.
2. Divide the participants into groups of four to six members.
3. Direct each group to combine their lists to write a short poem.
   (If there are six people in the group, there will be six nouns, six adjectives, etc.)
4. Ask the groups to read the final poem or post the poems for the class members to guess the authors. Surely, the results will be drastically different and unique.

VARIATIONS:

- **Music Poetry** Give specific guidelines to the students, such as only using words about composers, music composition, concert etiquette, music the choir is learning, or top '40s music. Urge the students to set their poem to a melody.
- **Christmas Carol Poetry** Each group writes new lyrics to a familiar holiday song using the directions above. The groups can perform their new and improved carol for the class or go caroling during an activity period or lunch time.

ICE TIPS:

- Supply ideas or concepts if a group has trouble coming up with a topic.
- Younger students can choose from a prepared list.
- This could be a cross-curricular exercise with the English department.
- This icebreaker works with all ages of students.
- Students who are a significant part of the process have ownership in the class.

commonalities

Building Respect – Valuing Every Person in the Room

PURPOSE:
This icebreaker explores the common interests and connections that class members share.

REQUIREMENTS:
None

PREPARATION:
None

DIRECTIONS:
1. Instruct the students to find a partner.
2. Inform the pairs that they have two minutes to discover three specific things they have in common. If both students like to read, they need to distinguish more specifics (both prefer romance novels, mysteries, biographies, etc.). If they both enjoy dessert, they need to agree on a specific dessert (chocolate is not an acceptable answer).
3. In the next round, combine couples so the two now becomes a group of four students.
4. Repeat the steps above until all four members agree on a commonality.
5. Repeat the process until the entire class reaches one specific commonality.

VARIATIONS:
- **Inside the Commons** Students stand in one circle. If they answer "yes" to a series of questions, they move to the middle of the circle. The questions can range from silly to serious (e.g. Can you can tie a bow tie? Can you make motorboat sounds with your lips? Can you touch your nose with your tongue?).
- **Musical Commonalities** See if the class can agree on musical topics (e.g selection, performer, conductor, style, or music hall).

ICE TIPS:
- Challenge the group to put careful thought into their commonalities. "Music" would not be an acceptable answer because all of the students in your choir or ensemble have music as a common interest.
- Fostering feelings of trust and acceptance is difficult when a student doesn't know or understand fellow classmates.
- A student may discover another person in the class who shares the same hobbies, talents, and passions.

i spy in the classroom

Building Respect – Valuing Every Person in the Room

PURPOSE:

I Spy in the Classroom requires students to secretly observe and report on the good rehearsal etiquette of the person whose name that they drew.

REQUIREMENTS:

Container

Slips of paper with students' names listed

Pen or pencil

PREPARATION:

List each student's name on a slip of paper.

DIRECTIONS:

1. Allow each student to draw a slip of paper that lists another student's name.
2. Advise the students that the objective of this game is to observe and report good behavior in rehearsals. The students should be hyper-focused as they "spy" on the positive actions of another classmate. Teach students to look for the best in their classmates and require them to list only positive statements. Tell the students that "nothing" will not be an acceptable answer.
3. Allow time at the end of class for students to write down and hand in the good behavior reports of their chosen student.
4. Display the positive behavior slips or reward the students who received exceptional reports. It is a huge boost of confidence for students to read positive statements about themselves.

VARIATION:

I Spy Rewards Sweeten the deal - reward the student with the best report a prize. Another award might be giving the winner the authority to choose the closing activity, instructing the teacher to put away folders, or observing the rehearsal from the choir director's location. At the end of the month or semester, put all the positive behavior students' slips into a hat and draw one name for a big prize package. Students who had several reports of positive behavior will have a greater chance of winning.

ICE TIPS:

- Practicing good behavior in a game can turn into daily good habits.
- Students work harder and are conscientious knowing someone is observing.
- Remind the students that while they are observing a fellow classmate, someone is also watching them to report on their actions.

take a stand

Building Respect – Valuing Every Person in the Room

PURPOSE:
Every person has different opinions on various topics. This icebreaker encourages the students to take a stand, as well as get a sense of their classmates' positions on various matters. It is healthy for students to see the diversity of their peers and that the mixture of various personalities is beneficial to the team.

REQUIREMENTS:
A roll of masking tape or a long rope

List of questions for students to *Take a Stand*

PREPARATION:
Move the chairs and other items to the outside of the classroom to create a large open area. Use masking tape or a rope to create a long line down the center of the classroom.

DIRECTIONS:
1. Inform the students that you will read a series of questions aloud to them. The topics range from serious to silly.
2. Challenge them to consider the questions and take a stand when giving answers. There are no right or wrong answers in this icebreaker. When the students decide their position, they should move to the designated area that best represents their answer. For example, call out "dogs or cats?" Those participants that prefer dogs move to one side of the tape and those that prefer cats move to the opposite side of the line. If a student cannot make a choice, instruct the student to straddle the tape line.

    Ideas for *Take a Stand* icebreaker:
    - Regular or diet soda?
    - Spiders or snakes?
    - Milk chocolate or dark chocolate?
    - Republican or Democrat?
    - Football or basketball?
    - Running or walking?
    - Country or pop music?
    - Dance or sing?
    - Boxers or briefs?
    - Chick flicks or horror films?

ICE TIP:
Urge the students to brainstorm their own topics for *Take a Stand*. Ask volunteers to call out categories.

ICEBREAKERS

attitude game

Building Respect – Valuing Every Person in the Room

PURPOSE:
This icebreaker helps people prepare to deal with a variety of situations in a positive manner by contributing ideas of how to react positively and negatively in situations.

REQUIREMENTS:
Paper

Writing Utensil

PREPARATION:
Different lists of five attitude statements for each group (see samples below)

DIRECTIONS:
1. Divide the students into groups of four to six people.
2. Distribute a different list to each group.
3. Ask a volunteer from each group to serve as secretary and read the statement aloud.
4. Permit the students to discuss a negative (wrong) reaction and a positive (correct) reaction while the secretary takes notes.
5. Call upon each group to present its responses to the rest of the class.
6. Discuss why positive reactions are essential to the success of the ensemble.

Possible statements to discuss in *Attitude Game*:
- The group did not receive the desired rating at the state music festival.
- The holiday concert was cancelled due to weather.
- The piano is not in tune.
- A member of the choir forgot his uniform and music folder on the bus.
- The same people seem to get many of the solos.
- The choir members are tired of rehearsing the same section of music.
- You feel you have better ideas than the director, choreographer, or accompanist.
- You are accused of talking during rehearsal when it was your neighbor.
- The same people are in the front row on the risers again.
- You must share a music folder with someone who sings off key.

VARIATION:
Role-play Attitude Game Instruct the groups to role-play their negative and positive reactions to each situation. Each group should close with the positive scenario.

ICE TIPS:
- This icebreaker prepares students of what is acceptable behavior in certain scenerios.
- Emphasize and encourage the positive.
- Encourage all students to contribute by adding their thoughts and ideas.

say "oh!"

Building Respect – Valuing Every Person in the Room

PURPOSE:
Students will listen to vocal inflections and watch body language.

REQUIREMENTS:
None

PREPARATION:
A list of sentences (see below)

DIRECTIONS:
1. Split the students into two groups.
2. Instruct the students that as the statements are read aloud, the first group responds to each sentence with the verbal response of "Oh!" The second group refrains from responding and listens to the vocal inflections of the first group.

Sentences to use in *Say Oh!*:
- My dog died
- Look at that cute baby
- Drink this sour lemonade
- Your math quiz was graded and you forgot to do the back page
- You are the winner of the $100,000,000 sweepstakes
- Your best friend and her boyfriend broke up
- Dad is wearing his embarrassing Hawaiian shirt in public again
- Look at that girl in the short mini-skirt (split the boys and the girls on this one for their different reactions)

VARIATION:
Visual Say Oh! Challenge the students to use only facial gestures (no verbal).

ICE TIPS:
- Discuss how listening and speaking affect communication.
- Send the right signals when healthy communication is desired. Openness sets the tone for a dialogue.
- Hear what people are saying as well as what they are not saying.
- Discuss leaders who embody positive communication skills and how their listening and speaking skills have a bearing on their leadership status.
- Let your actions speak for themselves. And only when necessary, use words.

ICEBREAKERS

Building Respect – Valuing Every Person in the Room

PURPOSE:
As students present objects they value, their classmates gain a greater understanding about each person.

REQUIREMENTS:
None

PREPARATION:
On a designated day, ask students to bring three to five items from home that have a significant meaning and represent what is valuable in the student's life (photos of family, friends, and pets, stuffed animals, CDs, poetry they composed, clothing items, or childhood toys, etc.). Ask them to place the items in a sack or box to keep them hidden until time for the presentations.

DIRECTIONS:
1. Either ask the students to present to the entire group or divide the participants into smaller groups.
2. One by one, each student shares their prized items and explains the significance of why each items is important to them.

VARIATIONS:
- Students share their favorite music or song with the class. Inform students that the language and content must be suitable by school rules.
- Play excerpts of several styles of music and ask the group for feedback. (One style of music will be one person's favorite and may be his classmate's least favorite). Since every ensemble or team has varying ranges of diversity, the students will acknowledge and hopefully appreciate the differences.

ICE TIPS:
- Instructors should give the students plenty of notice about this activity.
- This icebreaker works great for a retreat or a special rehearsal.
- Point out that this icebreaker is an exercise in life values and respect. What may be important to one person may not be to another. Students need to hold each member of the ensemble in high esteem.
- Remind students to demonstrate respect during the presentations as they too will present their valued objects.
- Discuss how the world would be a boring and monotonous place if people were the same.

encouraging words

Building Respect – Valuing Every Person in the Room

PURPOSE:
Encouraging Words is a tremendous boost of affirmative words and positive reinforcement for students. The end result of a bookmark is a tangible reminder of their classmates' kind words.

REQUIREMENTS:
Light-colored construction paper (8 1/2" x 11")

Felt tip pen or fine tip markers in various colors

Laminator (optional)

PREPARATION:
Cut the paper in half-length wise to create a 4 1/4" x 11" piece.

DIRECTIONS:
1. Ask the students to sit in a circle after choosing a colored piece of paper and several writing utensils.
2. Inform the students to print their names neatly and boldly on the top of the bookmark.
3. Instruct students to pass their paper to the person to their immediate right. After the pass, the receiver reads the name of the person and writes a positive note, phrase, word, or memory about the person on the sheet of paper. Encourage the students to give serious thought to the individual and his special talents.
4. Set a time limit. At the end of the allotted time, the students pass the papers again to the right and repeat the process. Note: If you allow one minute for each person and you are working with a group of 50 students, this icebreaker will take approximately one hour.
5. After the final person has written his comments, collect the bookmarks (without allowing the students to read the statements) to laminate for longevity. This is a good way to ensure all the comments are encouraging and uplifting. Save the bookmarks until a special event or a time that the students need a pick me up.

VARIATION:
Depending on how extravagant you want to be, consider a range of materials to autograph (T-shirts, posters, programs, even old dance shoes can make special memories). The students can add their own special touches with musical stickers or with a star or heart shaped hole-puncher.

ICE TIPS:
- *Encouraging Words* icebreaker is one of the best "feel-good" motivational activities available. It also has long lasting benefits as students have a tangible keepsake that reinforces positive qualities.
- Instructors spend sufficient rehearsal time correcting and dealing with an ensemble's mistakes. This can take a toll on the student. This activity allows students to recognize their significance and contribution to the ensemble.

ICEBREAKERS

ICEBREAKERS